Laurie's Bundle of Poetic Humour

Laurie Wilkinson
The Psychy Poet

‘Laurie is a poet who gets to the heart of the matter. His verses touch all our lives, and like himself, gives us great joy even in the dark days.

Published in UK in 2021 by BadGoose Publishing.

ISBN: 9798755274951

Cover Photo: Jester

Thanks for cover profile pictures to:

Sylvie Blackmore - BBC Radio Sussex & Surrey
Mick Seaman - Retired
Liz Pellet - Manager Seabreeze Cleaning Ltd
Sandra Da Silva Creasey - Pink Spaghetti P A Services

Cover Design by: James Harvey.

Introduction

Following on very quickly from my ninth book "Our World in Verse", this poetic offering is very different in as much that it only has the one subject, Humour. This is the "best of" from all my previous books and seems to be a very popular idea, (initially raised by my publisher and website guru James Harvey).

We checked people's thoughts and opinions, and as the feedback was positive here is an all humour poetry book to help cheer everyone up a bit. There is even more than a suggestion that my "Best of Romance" may be waiting, (or should I say cuddling?), in the wings

This book has 76 of my amusing poems from positive feedback that have been either; requested for repeat, abundantly popular at my reading and entertaining gigs, nominated as personal favourites or possibly striking an amusing chord along with general topical subjects for a laugh.

There are eight sections or categories for the poems spread across; pub themes, social behaviour, sexual involvements and the joys of technology. All touching on everyday stories and activities of life as well, so again something for everybody.

Naturally my two created mischievous teddy bears Ted and Beth have their own section on their antics and naughtiness, we can't help but love them.

Laurie Wilkinson

Please dive in and enjoy choosing your own favourite subjects or poems as The Journey Continues while still collecting for, and donating to, the excellent charity Help for Heroes that cares for our wounded."

Thanks and Best Regards,
Laurie Wilkinson Bsc (hons) RMN

To Fred & Nicola,
All Best Regards,
Laurie
Dec 2022

Acknowledgements

I need to state that as this is now my tenth book and thus the 10th Acknowledgements I have written, I am looking back over the history of all my books to recognise all the "help and support" I have had which seems to fall into two main forms.

One, the general advice, help, and encouragement to actually write, and two, the support, assistance and opportunities to promote and sell my books that donate to the excellent charity Help for Heroes that cares for our wounded.

The lists of all the people involved in the two points above could be almost endless, so I will just loosely touch upon key players and organisations here and thank the many others personally. Obviously over my eight publication years some folks have "come and gone" in the natural movements, involvements and flow of life.

Encouraging and advising on my writing mainly have been my, (now sadly late), wife Iris and our family, Elizabeth Wright (The Writer) who mentored and advised me from my very start. The Anderida Writers Eastbourne, "Poem Readers and Feedback Givers" who over time include; Diana M, Kelly B, Suanne P in S Africa, Shona in New Zealand, Deb B, Carol A, Sharon B. A work colleague from way back and now around Lesley A T among others not mentioned as per my comments above.

Alongside my, (often manic), efforts to promote me and my books have been; the wonderful Lyn Parsons of National Magic FM Radio with her endorsements, readings and mentions of me, the lovely Sylvie Blackmore of BBC Radio Sussex & Surrey, (photo on front cover), who has now had me as guest on her show many times to read my poems and talk about my poetry world, Simon Herbert of Hailsham FM for my regular guest slots, The 42nd Highland Regiment (1815) for support and buying my books, South East "Mumpreneurs" group, Hailsham Chamber of Commerce, The Sussex Newspaper Online for allowing my monthly column for over six years now, Seb and Team at Tesco Langley for allowing and helping my book sales and collecting for Help for Heroes, The Garden Bar Pub Eastbourne Waterside for continued support, and finally but not completely, Mick S and many friends on my, (now sold), static Mobile Home site in South West France.

As always my final recognition of gratitude is to you for taking the time to read my book and with even bigger thanks to the kind folks who have bought this book and perhaps my previous books too. I greatly appreciate this as it ensures the continuation of my donations to *Help for Heroes* from all sales made.

Thanks again, and bless you all!

Laughter

It's been said that if we try to laugh
The world will laugh with us too,
And I have always believed in this
So will mostly smile in all I do.

Because we must try to laugh at life
Even if we are losers or the winners.
Whether we're tall, short or maybe thin
Or those who never missed any dinners.

But it does always seem to be the case
That a smile or good laugh is catching,
So then it makes us feel much better
When our troubles we are despatching.

Contents

PUB

Bar Room Star

Every pub or bar will have one
There are lots of them about,
And while everyone likes talking
He feels the need to shout.

Amongst his group of cronies
He must be the loudest bloke,
Then burst into raucous laughter
Every time he cracks a joke!

I turn my head to see him
But you couldn't miss the noise,
For he's the best at shouting
In the group of loud old boys.

We all laugh at something
In our own personal way,
Within the bounds of reason
As appropriate for the day.

But this loud man doesn't realise
His grating voice won't nestle,
And he clearly has forgotten
The saying of the empty vessel.

So the loud man's noise continues
And his voice you couldn't douse,
Though I have a deep suspicion
That at home he's like a mouse!

--ooOoo--

Cocky Too's

Sitting on their bar stools
Just like parrots on a perch,
And delivering a sermon
As if they were in church.

Solving all the worlds deep problems
Without scarce a pause for breath,
It could be the beer talking
Or a latest script for meths!

My ears hear the words of wisdom
Spraying the bar room just like rain,
So I wonder why they're sat there
And driving everyone insane.

For if they have all the answers
To put all wrongs right,
Why not just go out and do it
And spare us all your sight!

Another correction to all errors
Follows a deep gulp of beer,
With a look that says I'm lucky
To be near enough to hear,
All the meaning of the mysteries
That world leaders cannot solve
Of poverty and pollution answers
That from this bar will evolve!

But I only went to the bar
To try to get myself a drink,
Past the barrier of "know all's"
That won't allow your brain to think
So I have my prudent answer
To the puzzle in my brain,
If I want peace and quiet
I won't come in here again.

--ooOoo--

Double Vision

I went into this village pub
For I was dying for a beer,
But I was very soon to learn
Not to ever come in here.

For I stood patiently at the bar
With a throat dry as a bone,
Despite coughing and shuffling
It seemed I was all alone.

But then a noise behind the bar
Caught both my ear and attention,
And with a very surprised eye
Saw the cause of service retention.
For the Landlady and barman both,
Were doing what comes naturally,
So I realised to my dismay
Neither would be serving me.

Now in a huff I went round the side
And entered the other bar,
But saw a barmaid and Landlord
In a clinch that went too far.

So storming out for another pub
That would hopefully quench a thirst,
I tripped over two copulating dogs
And furiously upon them burst,
With barely contained fury now
Complete with an angry frown,
I threw the randy dogs inside
Saying your ruddy sign fell down!

--ooOoo--

Badgers

There now appears to be a rash
Of job-description I D cards,
Worn proudly by those workers
Keen not to be seen as retards.

For they nobly masquerade now
Behind a "managers" badge bold.
Until of course you make a request
When they will just do as they are told,
By someone with a much larger badge
Or just metaphorically worn.
But clearly a step above the first,
Now gawping fish-like and forlorn.

At their forbidden rule to answer
The very simplest question asked,
But every dog must know its place
And not try to be multi-tasked.

I even see now that these cards
Are on ribbons dangled from the neck,
On view as a false security
For any requested check.

Though I really can't stop laughing
At such a futile little gesture,
For any would-be villain now
Couldn't be bothered to pester,
For a "Poundland" type of I D card
That could be "knocked up" in a shed.
As they would just hack the laptops
For any security breach instead.

But now even on holiday sites
Ribbon badges are flourished to see,
Exactly who has "weighed and paid"
But don't give one to me.

As I have never liked tick boxes
That we can all be placed in.
So carry my driving licence card
In my wallet, to avoid the sin,
Of a total non-conforming breed
Which may be a bridge too far.
But fear not for if I want something
I know exactly who you are!

--ooOoo--

Slow Hand George

There's a barman at the Garden bar
And "slow hand George" is his name,
For no matter if you're full or gasping
His manner's just the same.

No special favours or service
As he ponderously runs the bar,
With little acceleration shown
No matter who you are.
So many a dry throat croaks
Whilst waiting in his queue,
And you really fear you'll die here
Before he even gets to you.

But be re assured it's not personal
For every punters thirst will fall,
In the time "ol' slow hand" serves you
That's if you're even seen at all.
So as he shuffles to the end
Where the glass washing's done,
You wait until he comes back
Thinking a marathon he's run!

Though there is always hope here
That he will serve you in a trice,
As he has chatted up security
To run and get his ice.
And of course another trick
To keep slow hand from sin,
Is knowing you will get served
When the barmaid wanders in.

But I mustn't be too scathing
About slow hands lack of go,
For as you hopefully walk in
George will always say hello,
And give a welcome smile
With occasional clever look.
But I must confess I like him,
And he's even bought my book!

--ooOoo--

A Little Loud

A while ago I wrote a poem
Which was entitled "Bar Room Star",
All about a very loud man
I'd heard in a local bar.

But recently I have met his equal
In fact he really is much worse,
With his "over the top" loud voice
That could make a vicar curse.
And I know I have said before
That I can be loud as well,
But nobody could ever equal him
With his mouth almighty hell.

Strangely he is not very big
But you wouldn't think that the case,
For the cacophony of noise he makes
Could be heard in outer space.
So no, not really very tall,
Though he has a cocky manner,
Flowing from his jaunty frame
You'd love to hit with a spanner.

Thus if a shouting contest started
I could probably hold my own,
Whist accepting I could be beaten
By blokes of twenty stone.
Though as I said he's only small
But will always be the noisy winner,
For compared to all his shouting
Anyone else is a beginner!

--ooOoo--

Benefit of Laughing

Laughter rings across the room
Then there's shouts and cheers,
I look towards the revellers
Surrounded by their beers.

It is great to hear the laughing
Silence bettered by the noise,
So I smile back at the cheering
And the grown up girls and boys.

But something doesn't seem right
The laughter's much too fake,
It seems like a competition
And to shout for shouting sake.

Then the raucous noise is louder
By some banging on the table,
And each person sitting round it
Talks as loud as they are able.

If you didn't look too closely
At the total lack of grief,
You wouldn't see their fatness
Or distinctive lack of teeth.

What is this place I've come to?
It just does not seem the same,
As other pubs I've been to
So I will note the name!

A visit out to the toilets
Leaves me a bit perturbed,
Two men talk loudly at me
And I can't make out a word!

They seem to be quite happy
When they stagger out the door,
And roll towards their table
But one collapses on the floor.

This brings more fits of laughter
Though the bloke looks in distress,
But the revellers don't notice
That he's now a beer soaked mess.

On returning from the toilet
I have a look around the room,
At smaller groups of people
Sitting quietly as the tomb.

So I think I've got the answer
To the revellers all at play,
And their cause for celebration
Is that it is benefits pay day!

--ooOoo--

Scott or Not

Down my local is "Scott or not"
As I name his lack of recall,
For if someone's bin in asking
For you, he won't know at all.
So learning who the person was
Or what they had to say,
Will never be known by you
After an hour, let alone a day.

For Scott who forgets has issues
As he puffs upon his pipe,
As he politely tells you now
That he is not a memory type.
So of course I must now wonder
When he cycles off to roam,
And rides his bike for miles
How the hell does he get home?

For a homing pigeon he is not
With an elephants memory,
So please don't leave a message,
If you want to contact me.
Though an idea would be a note
With my contacts on a chit,
But as sure as eggs are eggs
"Scott or not" will then lose it!

But be assured he can always
Pull a pint without delay,
And despite his dodgy recall
He won't forget you have to pay.
Though I'll say Scott has helped me
And in a big way as it goes,
Promoting me, and buying books
Which supports Help for Heroes!

--ooOoo--

SOCIAL BEHAVIOUR

Chariot Wheels

Shopping trolleys are inanimate
I want to make that clear,
They really cannot be blamed
If pushed by a Boadicea

Waddling largies push these carts
Like Rommel with his tanks,
And should you be in line of attack
You must dodge with little thanks.

Whether you are in or out the store
The dangers just the same,
Except inside there is little room
And much less chance to complain.

Outside in the widespread terrain
Your worry is their speed,
Or the lack of route or direction
So look out or you will bleed!

Propelled with gusto by the hulks
They roar across the road,
And doesn't need a genius to see
They don't know the Highway Code.

The shopping trolley chariot race
Should fill your heart with fear,
For driven by these Amazon's
Even Ben Hur would not go near!

So stepping back inside the shop
You should feel no need to beg,
Until an unseeing Genghis Khan
Shoves their trolley in your leg.

Little old ladies are just as bad
And be sure you are no freer,
For they've no idea where to push,
And you they can't see or hear.

These rattling supermarket trains
That is the shoppers trolley,
In themselves are little threat
Only when trundled by a wally,
Of whom there seems to be a horde
Not knowing where there going,
And don't see or care for us
Who risk all by our unknowing.

That to survive the trolley dash
You must forget all manners,
And do your very best to avoid
Trolley chariots and their banners!

--ooOoo—

Coughs and Colds

Coughs and colds will drive us mad
And surely catch us on the run,
For in winter, summer, rain or dry
They're sure to stop and spoil our fun.

A streaming cold and sneezes too
Will turn your nose into a beetroot,
And bleary eyes and banging head
Tells you that you have a real brute.

Coughing up when you try to breathe
And unable to speak clearly any more,
Are symptoms of the dreaded cough
With each hack painfully sore!

These nasty bugs will lay you low
Whatever relief you try to pursue,
A common cold the girls call it
But to most men it's a "man flu".

Coughs and colds will drive us mad
And surely catch us on the run,
For in winter, summer, rain or dry
They're sure to stop and spoil our fun.

So tickling cough and running nose
Will make you feel a bit like a leper,
And episodes of your sneezes
Seems as if you've snorted pepper!

So don't be dismayed about feeling bad
With watery eyes and head like glue,
For though small consolation that it is
Surely everyone will catch it too!

--ooOoo—

Bladdered?

Gosh my bladder is so full
It won't hold another drop,
But I'm driving with my legs crossed
And can't find a place to stop.

My concentration is steadily going
I can barely think straight at all,
And I must answer this urgent message
Or I will soon be sitting in a pool
Of escaping heated liquid,
Crying that it needed release.
So I must relieve myself somewhere
For mind and body are craving peace.

I then turn off into a back street
But no handy trees or fields are here.
Thus I get on my knees behind the door,
So my actions are not clear
To anybody who looks my way,
Who can't see if I'm there or not.
And again I count my blessings
That I have no need to squat!

Oh what is it with our bladder?
That it remains calm without a need
To be emptied for many long hours,
But other times requires top speed.
Then it seems you have only just been
To do what your body commands,
And before you can relax carefree
It again makes its demands.

Psychologists think they have the answer
And are certain that they know,
The more you think about your bladder,
It will increase the need to go.
But I'm not convinced that's right,
Though it could just be me,
Who thinks the further from a toilet
Will bring on the need to pee.

So that's the conundrum of the bladder
And complex without a doubt.
But one thing we know for sure is,
That what goes in comes out!

--ooOoo–

Fish on a Bike

Some images are just too implausible
Yet we often use them to give a view,
Of a ridiculous descriptive point
That any sane mind won't pursue.

Like the saying of a fish on a bike
Or the proverbial bag of snakes,
Which we all know is a bit bizarre
But as counter argument often makes,
Reinforced improbability of someone
Doing the job just as you would like.
So the chance of that ever happening,
Is as likely as a fish riding a bike.

Thus we use many florid descriptions
Mostly in a reverse psychology way,
Like people "useful as a chocolate teapot",
And such sayings will brighten our day.
For a heavy downpour or rainstorm
Is described as raining cats and dogs,
And just who can forgot an odd person
Said to be as mad as a box of frogs?

There are lots of other sayings as well
Adding more colour to what we say,
Like in taking advantage of opportunity
And when the sun shines make our hay,
Which is probably quite an old suggestion
Going right back to our language roots,
Such as when things are all going well
We're advised to go fill our boots.

Getting "into the swing" with this now
I could possibly cover more ground,
Which brings another saying to mind
And that is as "sound as a pound".
For saying people are daft as a brush
Or blind as a bat, can add to the log,
And may lead to someone who is ill
Being described as sick as a dog.
Thus it seems the list is quite endless
Almost as far as the eye can see.
But I don't want to make a mistake,
And go barking up the wrong tree.

So best I end this ode of sayings now
Or else go on like "Tennyson's Brook",
Though I'm quite sure it will amuse you
And be noted as worth a second look.
For you might keep your eyes peeled
Or be dry as a bone, is another I like.
But I must admit my favourite saying,
Is that of the fish riding a bike.

--ooOoo—

Late

The clock is ticking past the time
That you had agreed to meet,
And nobody has called round yet
So you begin to fidget in your seat.

You start to think and ponder
If the right time is in your head,
But you can only convince yourself
Of the time that you both said.
So if believing that you are right
Perhaps they must have got it wrong,
Though one thing now is certain
Is that you can't wait too long.

For today with all our technology
Any communication is very easy.
With a phone call, text or message,
But getting nothing makes you queasy.
So you start marching all around
Making little circles on the floor.
Whilst getting more worried and anxious
As still nobody is at the door.

Again you ring their numbers
But no answering voice replied,
It just seems you're getting snookered
With everything done or tried.

The agreed time is now well past
And arrangements are up the wall.
Until double checking your diary
And start to feel an utter fool.
For there should be no one coming
Though the agreed time is as you state,
But the answer to your frustrations
Is that you have the wrong date.

--ooOoo—

Dancing

Many people like to have a dance
And I did quite a bit as well,
But largely just ballroom and Latin
Although maybe you couldn't tell.

For you don't just need to be tall
With that lean and angular pose,
As the majority who socially dance
Don't have figures much like those.
But that doesn't matter too much
As the biggest thing is enjoyment,
But some people think they're good
With dancing skills heaven sent.

Though others will just plod along
As they trundle round the hall,
With movements that clearly show
They have no rhythm at all.

Now just to demonstrate that point
Some dances change partners around,
With a variety of different couples
Not so sure of where they're bound.

And of course there are large people
Who struggle to keep steps flowing,
So with your eyes in a ladies chest
You can't see where you are going,
With the music unable to give a clue
As you waddle round in great fear,
For lost in a ladies large bosom
The music you cannot hear.

But it was not always like that
As I tried hard for perfection,
Though that didn't come easily
Often calling for some correction,
To my posture and general bearing
On professionals so easily seen.
But I used to quite enjoy myself
As a dancing king with a queen.

--ooOoo—

Mr. Splash

I call myself mister splash
And I just really cannot stop,
For however careful that I am
I always spill things with a plop.

Not like I'm dropping everything
More of a sort of splash about,
Like wielding a watering can
When I always drop the spout.

Any nicely rubbed clean surface
All cleared and wiped down dry,
Will soon be wet and soaking
When a tap jet makes water fly.

I can brew a lovely cup of tea
Even coffee I make well too,
But when walking to take it out
Then it will slop all on my shoe.

Washing up is nice and easy
And one of my usual chores,
But whilst all the cups are clean
There's water all on the floors.

Pouring water from the kettle
Into the cups and saucers there,
Often makes a messy splash
That makes me cuss and swear.

Taking tea bags from the cups
And to put out into the waste,
Will always splat on the table
As I drop them in my haste.

So I'm trying hard to be good
And not splash stuff everywhere,
By slowing myself down a bit
Will help me take more care!

--ooOoo—

Left Turn Loons

We all have odd bad driving moments
But some seem totally on the moon,
And one of the very worst of these
Is the really annoying left turn loon.

Now most idiotic, or just lazy drivers
Who won't or can't bother to indicate,
Are an absolute pain in themselves
But morons not showing left complicate,
One of the simplest driving manoeuvres
That even the daftest driver can do,
Yet failure to complete this social task
Will greatly frustrate me and you.

Because as directed in the highway code
We give way to traffic coming right,
Thus we obediently sit to allow this
As non-indicating cars turn out of sight.
For if they had been in any way caring
They would indicate left as they approach,
But as they turn left giving no signal
Their lack of consideration we reproach.

For as we just sit there in frustration
Having missed a safe chance to pull out,
The selfish idiot will drive carelessly on
Wondering what your wave is about.

But I guess no increased car technology
Can eradicate the berk behind the wheel,
For even if they had ability to notice
I suspect they wouldn't care or feel,
That they've been ignorant and selfish
And their driving is like a poor joke.
So our moronic cretin continues on
Without considering other folk.

--ooOoo—

Trolley Folly

Some people walk slow, others fast
A few may have no choice,
But let them have a shopping trolley
And it becomes their own Rolls Royce!
So like the old fairground ride
With banging, crashing, bumper cars,
Pushing at their precious trolley
Their heads among the stars.

It's my box of space, they seem to say
When clearly getting in the way,
But it has to be the greatest sin
If you should move their trolley in,
And a protective glare is hurled at you
Don't touch my trolley whatever you do.
For if across an aisle like a barricade
It's your fault, and the move you made!

But worse, oh so much worse than this
Is the one, who cannot push or steer,
As you've no chance of avoiding them
However much you try to keep clear.
For with eyes glued on a mobile phone
Or an "oldie" trying to read their list,
It will be more by luck than judgement
That your flesh they've barely missed!

So some will push slow, others fast
But you have no chance of getting past,
For with shopping done, or not yet started
Unlike the Red Sea, they won't be parted
From the trolley front or even behind,
So it's like watching them walking blind.
But the biggest scare and for cover I dive
Is seeing them get in a car and drive!

--ooOoo—

Front Line Action

I don't want a pot belly
They say it comes with age.
Looking at some younger folk,
It seems they're all the rage!

Is it the booze that causes it,
Or eating fast food take-aways?
But whatever the reason for it,
Should you get a "pot", it stays.

It's said that if you eat too much
The weight goes to your tum.
But I think that's only half of it,
It's also sitting idle on your bum!

Few people want to walk much
So they stand at the taxi rank,
Or drive just a few yards or so
In a giant motor, like a tank.

I don't like my pot that's there
Just above my trouser line.
But I must admit to feeling smug,
If they're over twice the size of mine.
And back sides too, are getting big,
In those outsize clothes they pack
Those very large and active cheeks,
Like two pigs playing in a sack.

So it's food, drink and sitting down
Too much, that all causes growth.
With lots of people waddling round,
Having one big leg the size of both.

But one thing has come to our aid
In the shape of big electric carts,
That carry heavyweights around
With all of their out sized parts!

--ooOoo—

Deposit Account

There is something in the toilet
That just won't go away,
Everyone can see it
But no one wants to say.

That this object just sits there
Looking very much like a log,
And somehow it remains
So you want to blame the dog,
For making this large deposit
In the urinal systems bank,
But wherever it came from
It's starting to smell rank.

Has someone not ate beans
Or taken tablets of iron?
Because it's getting nasty
And could now scare off a lion.

We've tried giving it a prod
And covering with some bleach,
Though it really is resistive
Like something beers can't reach.

But finally it goes away
And that's the end of that,
So now we will have to keep
A watch on the blooming cat!

--ooOoo—

But

Though only a very small word
It can work just like a tut.
When people say one thing
And then change it with a 'but'.
For example you may often hear
"I don't want to pry or be rude"
But then they proceed verbally,
To be offensive and intrude.

"I really didn't want to say anything
But then just felt I had to",
And they continue to comment
On all that you say or do.
Another example is semi praise
That can initially sound nice,
Like "I thought you were very good
But you need to practice once or twice".

So if people are thinking something
And know what they want to say,
Why the need to use the 'but' word
Before saying it anyway?

"Oh and it's really not my business
But thought I should make you aware",
And then go on and advise you
Whilst fixing you with a stare,
Which shows just that they think
The opposite to what they said.
For believing it does concern them,
You should do it their way instead.

So that is my little comment
And the subject I will shut,
For I have nothing more to say
And don't want to upset you, 'but'!

--ooOoo--

STORIES

Bear in the Window

The teddy bear was hanging
By its neck inside the shop,
So I walked right in to tell them
That I had to make it stop.

A woman came to serve me
So I pointed out their fault,
That a Teddy bear was suffering
And by the neck was caught.

I really did not like to see it
And little kids would be dismayed,
To see that such a cuddly toy
Was so callously displayed.

I again told them the problem
And in a shop for charity,
A bear suspended by the neck
Was not very nice to see!

Trying to use some humour
And to get right to the nub,
I told them I was chairman
Of the "Bears protection club"

The woman looked quite shaky
And could tell that I was right,
That in a shop front such as this
Should not be a grisly sight.

A manager was called to see me
From a room right out the back,
Who very soon agreed with me
That she could get the sack,
For not seeing the situation
Or the teddy bears upset,
And very quickly released him
Saying she was in my debt!

Then starting from tomorrow
She would change the shop around,
Ensuring that all teddy bears
Would then be safe and sound.

Now if there's a moral to this story
It's that we must learn to care,
For each and every one of us
Starting without teddy bear!

--ooOoo—

Humpty Dumpty Revisited

Most people know about Humpty Dumpty
But how many know the story facts?
And maybe wonder why he sat on a wall
With a shell that so easily cracks.
And was it partly his obese type figure
That rendered him in danger to fall,
For surely he should have thought
He might easily slip off the wall?

And then the involvement of kings men
Who were presumably meant to guard,
And not fuss over an accident prone egg
So perhaps they didn't try too hard
To put his pieces back together again,
And cleaned up helped by their horse.
Who really had no choice in all this,
But then you guessed that of course?

Now onto the popularity of Humpty
Among the townsfolk needing to beg,
For food, money and other problems
And no time to worry over an egg,
Who apparently never did much work
Perhaps explaining why he was fat.
Because we need exercise and labour
And not just sit on a wall like that!

So on thinking about what happened
To cause him being put back together,
After his famous "egg stravigant" fall
Which really wasn't that clever.
For the working folk of the kingdom
Are all really now tired and bushed,
So that brings me to the conclusion
The unpopular Humpty was pushed!

--ooOoo—

Nellie and I

Nellie and I met out in Thailand
That I can never quite forget,
Along with other memories
On an island called Phuket.

We had gone to a safari centre
All proceeds to help animals there,
So I was really happy to note
An impressive level of care.
Especially the elephants at risk
All treated nicely and well fed.
With lots of activities to do,
Or be hunted outside instead.

So off on an elephant ride then
We travelled all over the park,
To see the animals at their rest
So no poachers could leave a mark.
Soon it was time for the animal show
The elephants showing what to do,
Like how to play games and football
And coming to meet me and you.

Then it came to the show's highlight
People would lay flat like on a rack,
And an extremely large elephant
Put his foot almost on your back.
Delighted squeals and thumbs up
When punters went up one by one,
As if they were to be squashed
By this animal of many a ton!

Then they called for a volunteer
My wife pushed me to the fore,
To get a real close up of Nellie
Though I wasn't really too sure.
But the staff quickly took over
Saying you sir please lay face up,
Oh joy, I was getting a clear view
But I didn't want to win this cup.

Then the girls had soon taken over
Making me lay flat like on a bunk,
Slipping bananas up my shorts
Nellie would get back with her trunk.
But of course I didn't know this
So that I wasn't thinking too much,
That a banana seeking Nellie
Would trunk grope up my crutch.

Well obviously I was very surprised
As I really didn't have a clue,
That when being pressed to stardom
Just what our big Nellie would do.
So I had to just burst out laughing
At this massive shock of mine,
Not expecting an elephants trunk
Up where the sun won't shine!

--ooOoo—

Guardian Angel

To keep me out of trouble
I have a guardian angel bold,
Who makes sure I toe the line
And do exactly as I'm told.

So I should stay completely safe
And on the straight and narrow track,
For with my lookout and adviser
Someone always has my back,
To ensure that from any problems
I am always free, and safely steered,
As my angel will redirect me
If any wrecking rocks are neared.

Thus I had set out in life
Confident I would commit no crime,
Like falling foul of Albatross
Or talking loudly all the time!
So my conscience would be clear
My character wouldn't have a stain,
And if invited out for dinner
I'd have an invitation back again.

But oh, I did get in some mischief
And into major problems I did leap,
So why didn't my angel protect me?
Because the bugger had fell asleep!

--ooOoo—

Ritual Dance

Performing in many offices or workplace
Dashing in and out of meetings too,
You can easily see the peacocks
Strutting in front of me and you.

For they're puffed up with importance
Believing they are the very best,
Though fail to see the world will turn
After they're finally laid to rest.

With manic excesses, that won't be long
When combined with a ritual dance,
Like some sad, lovelorn peacock
Caught up in egotistic trance.

So extended beyond any competence
With their arrogance on show,
Masking and covering ignorance
That they don't seem to know.

For this presumption and conceit
Manifests right across their game,
So not seeing any shortfalls
They just remain the same.

Thus on and on goes their dance
With energetic, ignorant bliss.
Which slowly drains wasted days
Until death's angel plants her kiss!

--ooOoo—

Toilet Rolls

The simple and humble toilet roll
Has so very quickly now become,
That much more than a commodity,
We use to carefully wipe our bum.
Because in this world wide virus panic
The population has begun to stockpile,
And seemingly our toilet roll paper
Is wanted for a very long while.

Now to be honest I can't easily see
That faced by a deadly viral strain,
What having a stockpile of bog rolls
Can begin to help you survive again.
For there are many more basic needs
Required to ensure you stay well,
And protect you and all your family
From this creeping menaces hell.

But if it makes you feel much better
About all that might happen to you,
Get using all those stored toilet rolls
To gratuitously wipe your botty poo.
For perhaps it is your edgy nerves
Causing mega action of your bowels,
So you need to have plenty of paper
And not have to use your towels.

Of course you can feel really smug
If having a large toilet roll mound,
When most of the people have none
And search for where they're found.

But without doubt your selfish shopping
Has ensured that there is a shortage now,
For you've successfully cleared the shelves
Which has made the general public vow,
To do exactly the same as you have done
So will also stock up for many a year.
Just because you totally lost your bottle
And need to constantly wipe your rear.

Now if there is any moral for all this
And your actions we try to understand,
We all wish your toilet paper is so thin
It ensures you get a poopy hand.

--ooOoo—

YOGA

To perform yoga is intriguing
So try it if you dare,
You sit, or lay upon a mat
And puzzle what goes where!

And when you have successfully,
Tied yourself up quite a lot,
Not moving, so it's hard to see,
If you're still alive or not?

But to help you with your yoga
And some of the pain relieve,
You lie very calm and silent,
While you still attempt to breath.

Try another skill of balance
Up on one leg, and smile,
Just practice you can do it,
But it may take quite a while!

There are though, other postures
When you just lay back and rest,
And after all the spasms,
You will like this bit the best.

Lay back and check your breathing
Going slowly in and out,
Surprisingly you feel good
And all relaxed without a doubt.

For those ancient yoga masters
Must have known just what to do,
About being calm and supple,
And living on past ninety two!

--ooOoo—

Sample

At certain ages our NHS
Want to do tests on us,
They say that they're simple
And sure to cause no fuss.
Well it said that in my letter
That came with all the kit,
To take the samples from me
To check that I was fit.

Now I do accept the importance
Of finding any "nasties" early,
But I really wasn't prepared
For the collecting hurly burly,
With the need to take samples
From a normal bodily motion.
Although it wasn't really that,
Causing the most commotion.

For the naturally passed stool
Mustn't touch the toilet water,
So you have to prevent this
In a battle with no quarter!

Thus I readily placed my trap,
That my clever brain had thought
Would do the job in hand,
But no motion did get caught.
For it was heavier than my tray
I had contrived to do the task.
So this job needs experience
But who the hell do you ask?

Well I decided there was nobody,
I could ask about catching poo.
So I had to rack my brains,
To see just what to do.
And the idea I had was good,
Putting something on the bend.
For I successfully caught my prize
That with my sticks I could attend.

So with a scrape at one end
And another bit from the rest,
I did this for the five days
Then sent away my test,
Sealed neatly in the little bag
And put in a post box near.
So you can imagine my relief
When my tests came back clear.

For it wasn't just the clean bill
My health had without stain,
More the great joy of not needing
To have to do it all again!

--ooOoo—

Little Things

Our life is full of irritations
Yes, they're mostly just a glitch,
But if they all go wrong together
It really can make life a bitch!

Any time you're in a hurry
And you need to be out the door,
Then you'll knock something over
And watch it spread across the floor.

Something slips out of your fingers
So you bend to get it back,
Only then you see and realise
It's fallen through the smallest crack.

Liquid can be really tricky
As you determine not to spill,
But sure as eggs are eggs
It is certain that you will!
And not a little drop of liquid
However the amount you've got,
For when "Murphy" makes the rules
You will spill the flipping lot!

Our life is full of irritations
Yes, they're mostly just a glitch,
But if they all go wrong together
It really can make life a bitch!

My main hated little nuisance
That can make me lose my rag,
Is anything you're moving
Will be sure to catch or snag.

These small things sent to try us
Like the little "three foot judge",
Ensure when undoing something
It will determine not to budge.

I guess the most famous hate
Is when buttering some bread,
And knowing that if you drop it
It will land on the side that's spread.

Our life is full of irritations
Yes, they're mostly just a pain,
But if they all go wrong together
They can make you go insane!

One sad fact that is for certain
Is that if you get cross and sore,
Those little things that bug you
Will just happen more and more.

So perhaps the best salvation
Is to seek refuge in your bed,
But if "Murphy" has his way again
You will just fall out on your head!

--ooOoo—

Fly Past

Flying creatures can be aggravating
And get you extremely mad,
Buzzing around and landing on food
Like an airborne "Jack the Lad".

Some can give you a sting as well
Filling many folks with dread,
That they will get a nasty prick
As they zoom around their head.
But flapping your arms all about
Won't work and can make you grieve,
For you will get stung for sure
If you trap one up your sleeve.

But what is it about those little flies
That makes us lose our wit?
Perhaps it's because they like poo
With a passion to roll in it,
And then eat some for a meal
For that's exactly what they do,
Ensuring that when they land on us
It can make us want to spew.

Though one special annoying thing
Is that persistent little fly,
Who however many times you swat
Just determines not to die.
So you flail your hands manically
Trying to give it a fatal crack,
But when you think you've got him
The blighter comes flying back.

--ooOoo—

O M G!

One of the most overused prattles now
Must be the "oh my god" saying,
Often said many times in a row
And has nothing to do with praying.
Probably another modern influence
That has been picked up here,
And garbled nonsensically too
In a manner not sincere.

Sometimes like a collective chorus
Uttered by a multi sized throng,
And certainly not an "hallelujah" one
Or Hebrew slaves going wrong.
But "oh my god" is now universal
And can be intoned at will,
Which will grate on sensitive ears
Far worse if the voice is shrill.

But I grew up with sayings too
Though I think much more in keeping,
To the area I came from
Where our humour wasn't sleeping.
Things like "oh stack me sweetly"
Have a more poetic ring,
Than the often repeated "oh my god"
That a tired boredom will bring.

So an exclamation of “Gordon Bennett!”
Or a rude one about “blue bums”,
For me have much more magic,
When out of my mouth it comes,
With another long term favourite
That has an amusing ring,
When shouted in pained frustration
You “cow son” blooming thing!

Thus I still believe the old gems
Will always be the best,
When “oh my god” has been forgotten
And can no longer pass the test,
Of muttered exclamations
When we're surprised or frustrated.
So keep those old sayings safe
As they really are gold plated.

--ooOoo—

I Wish I Could Whistle

I wish that I could whistle
Even if it wasn't quite in tune,
For when I purse my lips and blow
My cheeks swell like a balloon.

I used to be able to whistle a bit
Although in truth it was not great,
But I happily just blasted away
Until threatened with a fate
That was quite nasty and hostile
If I didn't stop my whistle shrill.
Which to me was disappointing
And like a very bitter pill!

For my dad was a terrific whistler
And could yodel properly too,
But my attempts were pretty sad
No matter what I tried to do.
So when I heard people sound
Their whistle heard near a mile,
I must admit to feeling envious
About my efforts so futile.

I watched people put two fingers
Past their lips and in the mouth,
And emit a screeching sound
That travelled north and south.
While others made less effort
For a shrill success as well,
But all my lip pursing efforts
Made my tongue hurt like hell.

So I could never be a wolf
Who whistled at girls passing by.
Though frowned on now to do that,
But I couldn't even try!

Thus I have given it up now
And will no longer try to blast,
My sound through lips and teeth
To come out slow or fast,
Or in fact make much of a noise
Leaving no doubts of my epistle,
That whilst not a bad bloke in life
He could never, ever whistle.

--ooOoo--

Bell End

I loved my football from an early age
And began to regularly go to matches,
Though being small and young in years
Often watched the games in snatches.
For in big crowds it was hard to see
Though you might be let down the front,
So I mostly got a good view
Amongst the crowds push and shunt.

Now I don't recall actually when
That I decided to get a bell,
Which I bought down the market
And it would raise devils in their hell.
Some people would have a rattle
Which made a clanking sound,
But I'm sure that Laurie's bell
Was heard all across the ground.

So I felt quite chuffed with this
Though I had begun to realise,
It wasn't popular with everyone
Because of its ring, and not the size,
Which wasn't that particularly big
But the clang was really loud.
Again not pleasing all about me,
Though I felt very proud.

The trouble, and the bells demise
Came about when we scored a goal,
In a very close, important game
So I rang out heart and soul.
But tragically I went too mad
And hit a big bloke in the face,
Who wasn't pleased and threatened
To put my bell up a personal place.

Thus that really spelt the sad end
Of me taking my bell with me,
As the crowd were mostly regulars
So the same people I would see.

Which invoked prudence over courage
Although I did think about a drum,
But I worried if I got one of those
The bloke might shove it up my bum.
So I decided to just shout out loud
Like others, who would also sing.
And though I still enjoyed myself
I really missed my bell to ring!

--ooOoo--

SEX

Naked Ambition

The shower setting at the gym
Is a place for communal undress,
With all kinds of behaviour
But perhaps some you should guess.

You can see all the different types
By their various mannerisms there.
For some are quite shy and bashful,
But others just stand and stare!

There is though one unwritten code
Whether you smile or wear a frown.
It says you can do much as you like
But you never ever look down.

Though some it doesn't seem to faze
As they swagger like a smiling punk.
I'm sure it wouldn't matter to them,
If they had a finger, or a trunk!

Others creep quickly out the shower,
A private person you'd have guessed.
It’s possible that they're very quiet
Or else not been well blessed.

The kingpin though, a man of brawn
Absolute content with what he's got.
But catching a glance in a mirror
It was surprisingly not a lot!

As for me with my large sized mouth,
I'm just happy to laugh with those.
Who also have no reason to brag,
But you'd not like it on your nose!

--ooOoo—

First Sex Lessons

We had no sex education at school
Or any that I can remember well.
Just about the gender differences
And hair growing where you tell,
What each other's parts look like
As there were no diagrams to see,
What boy and girls are like
And the different ways to pee.

We did have girls in my class though,
Who would pose and do their best
To help us, particularly Angela
Keen to show off her growing chest.
Though I wasn't too taken with it
Shown in the chemistry room with tubes,
For she was less impressively large
Than “Fat Barry's” large boy boobs!

But there was an unofficial lesson
Though it was actually called P T,
Where we had to strip off in the gym
And girls navy bloomers we could see.
Though again it made little impression
At my young and tender years,
But I have seen in much later times
They reduce some old men to tears.

Thus probably my main sex education
Was when older boys did arrange
A look at Janice the girl next door,
Though it all seemed rather strange,
When she pulled down her panties
To show us a hairy slope and mole.
But being football mad back then,
I failed to see another game and goal.

So that was all school days taught
On how these gender mysteries grow,
With odd things happening down there
That at first you didn't want to know.
So you just carried on with sport
Until soon needing to learn about
A growing interest in girls bodies,
With all the fun of finding out!

--ooOoo—

On or Off?

At those intimate moments in life
We have decisions that we might fear,
Such as when is the right time
To let those suitors extra near?

Maybe other little nagging worries
So you don't appear to cheat or con.
With that massive choice for men
About leaving those socks on.

Now these might seem quite simple
Little doubting thoughts and niggles.
But if arriving at inconvenient times
You won't welcome fits of giggles,
Coming loudly from your partner
That you really don't want to lose.
And you need so much to impress,
Rather than to puzzle, or amuse.

Now consideration must be given
On this great conundrum here,
So try to reduce embarrassment
And start with confidence, not fear.
But be very slow and careful
As you don't want to hear her mock.
So try to give a bit of thought
What to best do with your sock.

Now more of a decision for women
For men try their wicked way a lot.
Though how they made the lady feel
Will decide if she does or not,
Do that very precious human act
That in great emotion you can drown.
And how this plays out is simply,
If her drawers are up or down.

So back it comes to the dozy male
Trying not to make his lady scoff,
And believe me it is much preferred
To take those flipping socks OFF!

--ooOoo—

Knickers

Knickers are very evocative
And mean something to nearly all,
Though some people prefer them big
Whilst others like them small.

There are people always trying
To get in them, others out,
While bashful keep them firmly on
Many people will have a doubt,
Just which knickers to wear
Or even if they should,
Get into this undergarment game
If they intend to just be good.

And we must remember too
That advice given by our mums,
To always wear clean underwear
In case we show our bums,
After being in an accident
That can befall mankind,
But if you end up in hospital
There's much more on your mind.

For if this accident is very bad
And your brain now hardly flickers,
You'll have much more to worry about
Than the condition of your knickers.
Though in other situations
When you really can't be sure
If your luck is going to be in,
Less, could then be more.

So perhaps we should give more thought
About how our underwear fits,
Because it could be more important
Than just material to cover bits.

--ooOoo—

Up or Down?

There is a monumental dilemma
Which can make us smile or frown.
For it concerns the toilet seat
And should we leave it up or down?

Now this debate has run for years
And driven men and women apart,
Because there is no neutral ground
As opinions come from the heart.
For men will often lift the seat
But then neglect to put it back,
Which of course infuriates ladies,
So they will come out and attack.

But men say that they lift the seat
In an act of common courtesy,
As they don't want to be accused
Of spraying little drops of wee,
For not lifting up the toilet seat
Could risk it getting a trifle wet.
So if that's the unpleasant case
A damp bum is what you get.

Though ladies will argue their case
Of men's behaviour not being right,
And accuse them of being careless
If leaving the loo a messy sight.
For women continually say to men
That they need to try much more,
Not to leave seats up and damp
Or sprinkle on the floor.

Thus the argument still continues
And has done so much too long,
But I feel if leaving the seat down,
Men will still be in the wrong.
For it seems that there's no answer
Even if you fully use your wit,
But perhaps men should try harder
So women smile as they sit.

--ooOoo—

Diddler on the Roof

I could hear a sort of banging
That was to turn out exactly right,
But nothing causing the noise
Was at that point in my sight.

It seemed to come from next door
So for my neighbour I was concerned,
But any possible noise of her banging
Had many years ago been spurned.
So did she have workmen in
Knocking her fixtures all about?
Though on checking she was safe
I confirmed that she was out.

So this racket I couldn't ignore
Clearly came from another direction,
And was really beginning to bug me
Thus called for a closer inspection,
Of all around my own property
And so I looked about outside.
To be confronted by some seagulls
Making love with a fervent pride!

Therefore it really was a banging
Causing all the noisy din,
But gulls don't know the saying
About being better out than in.
For whatever the male was doing
To make his seagull lady squeak,
It was involved and very lively
All out action with his beak.

Now I'm really not a spoilsport
And everyone shows loving proof,
Of how they feel for their partner
But why choose my roof?

So showing my authority now
And that I could also bang,
I shut my garden box loudly
With a deep resounding clang,
To stop further amorous activity
And all romantic sorties,
Hoping this would now deter
Any future sexy naughties.

For if they really must continue
They can do so without fuss,
Or I will soon be teaching them
All about coitus interrupt us.

For I'm really not a spoilsport
With a stuck up manner all aloof.
And I understand you need love,
But not on my chuffing roof!

--ooOoo—

TED & BETH

Barely Heard

Ted and Beth are very happy
Content bears and not bores,
Only now there is a little problem
Beth has told me that Ted snores!

Ted of course he denies this
And says it's just not true.
Though actually I heard him,
Only that's between me and you.

Beth says she is quite desperate
To have a peaceful night.
For every time she drops off,
Ted's snort gives her a fright.

He says it's all an exaggeration
That many male bear's growl,
But Beth is getting very angry,
And may smother him with a towel.

Now there has to be a solution to,
This noise that comes from Ted.
For Beth states if it continues
He must sleep in the spare bed!

So that's the way they managed
With no arguments, no pain.
Until both of them got lonely,
And had to sleep together again.

Once more they are contented
Though Ted still makes a noise,
So Beth wears some ear plugs
Because he's best of Teddy boys!

--ooOoo—

Bears Bath Fun

Ted and Beth are full of fun
Happy bears and keen to laugh,
And one of their special joys
Is in a massive soapy bath.

With water sloshing everywhere
As the bath fills to the top,
Both laughing until they hurt
And their fur soaked as a mop.

Then Beth gives out a cry
As her paw's caught in the plug,
But again screams in surprise
As Ted frees her with a tug!

And so the bears fun continues
With the floor wet as it can be,
But their splashing just goes on
As if swimming in the sea.

Ted's got his toy boat in the tub
And Beth has her rubber duck,
But alas now their play fun
Is about to run out of luck.

For their big watery puddles
Are dripping through the floor,
But the bears still don't know it
Until a loud voice at the door,
Says "just what are you doing?"
An angry dad asks of the bears
Saying that all their splashing
Has made water leak downstairs!

So with a mop each in their paws
And a strong demand to sort it out,
Ted and Beth are now deflated
But will continue to muck about!

--ooOoo—

Can't "Bear" to Lose

Ted and Beth love their football,
And get behind the team they choose
When watching matches on the t v,
But are really grumpy if they lose.

They always pick a team to cheer
Whoever the two clubs that's playing.
No neutrality for either of them now,
For their pick to win they're praying.

Beth will choose her sides to support
For the looks and muscles of the teams,
But Ted goes for soccer skill and class
With the best tactics and schemes.
This is alright and fine of course
Unless their chosen teams oppose,
Then there'll be words and argument
That once so nearly came to blows!

But be assured Ted n Beth won't fight,
Of course like most couples they'll row.
And watching football is a powder keg
So to keep their peace they vow.

They do agree on one team though
Who they really love and cheer loudly,
It's the one their dad, The Psychy Poet
Always supported and watches proudly!

--ooOoo–

Bears Empty Promise

Who's been eating our porridge?
Ted n Beth would like to know,
When they come in for breakfast
After smelling food on the go.

But the porridge has all gone
The saucepan is scraped clean,
For though teddy noses smell it
There is nothing to be seen.
Only an empty dish and spoon
Still placed upon the table,
By another empty cookery jar
With “Porridge” spelt on the label.

This does not please our famous bears
Not one little bit at all,
For they're just beginning to rue
Not getting up on their first call,
When they decided to lay back
And have another little sleep.
With no thought of repercussions
That now makes them weep.

For the breakfast cook has done
And won't be making any more,
Of that delicious porridge
That most teddies will beg for.
And although the penny's dropped
They should have jumped out of bed,
Their dad has scoffed the porridge
So they will go without instead.

But Ted n Beth have both learned
A precious lesson so sublime,
And will make sure they're ready
For their breakfast the next time!

--ooOoo—

Tea for Two

Now Ted and Beth like a cup of tea
And will drink it all day long,
But both are reluctant to make it
So that's where it all goes wrong.

For Ted will say it's Beth's turn
She of course says it's Ted's,
So before you can say "teddy bear"
Another disagreement spreads
Into a mini bear fight,
Although they mean no harm.
For Beth will use her female wiles
And Ted will be all charm.

Thus often I am the peacemaker
And also the tea-making man.
Whilst they have their little bicker,
Though I suspect it's all the plan.
With a very cunning teddy ruse
To get me to make their drink,
But although I go along with it
I'm not as silly as they think!

For every time I make their tea
And we sit drinking with a chat.
I find out all their secrets,
How they got up to this and that.
For although they are a lovely pair
And our hearts they do enslave,
They can still be quite mischievous
So I make sure they behave.

Thus our little tea drinking parties
Have an agenda for me too.
As they help me keep a close eye,
On just what they plan to do!

--ooOoo—

Dental Bears

Poor Beth has got a toothache
And is in quite a lot of pain,
But she really is too frightened
To go to the dentist again.

Because the last time she went,
It wasn't very pleasant there.
As the dentist had no experience
Of tooth treatment for a bear!

Now Ted has said he will act
To get Beth's tooth out fast.
Which has filled Beth with terror
For Ted has tried this in the past,
When he put a string on his tooth
Attaching the other end to a door.
But instead of pulling his tooth out
It knocked him right onto the floor.

So this leaves Beth in a dilemma
Of what to do for the best,
To resolve her toothache problem
Which allows no peaceful rest.
For she is also getting grumpy
Ted says like a bear with a sore head,
But this doesn't amuse our Beth,
Who says she'll flatten him instead.

So there has to be an answer
And as usual Ted's his clever self,
When he went along to a library
To borrow a book off the shelf,
Which explains in great detail
And with photos in a sheath,
That he will show to the dentist
About treating teddy bear teeth.

--ooOoo—

Beth's Slippers

Beth bear likes carpet slippers
And loves to wear her mums,
But has to remove them quickly
Whenever her mum comes
Back into the house again,
From a trip to the local shop.
Beth knows she shouldn't do it
Though finds it hard to stop.

Now Ted has told Beth off
About her foot comfort greed.
Saying bears don't want footwear,
Though Beth just finds the need
To feel those comfy slippers
All warm around her paws,
But wouldn't wear them outside
As they're only for indoors.

But Beth got a big shock
When next the slippers wore,
For they were worn and smelly
And can't be put on any more.
So she whispered to her dad
To give mum a special treat,
And buy brand new slippers
For the comfort of her feet.

So Beth's mum now has new ones
Nice and comfortable to wear,
That although meant for humans
Are most appealing to our bear.
Though Beth now has to be good
And for her naughtiness atone,
But I hate to see her unhappy
So bought a pair to be her own.

--ooOoo—

Nimble Paws

Now despite being quite mischievous
Some things Ted and Beth keep quiet.
As they like to have some secrets
And not always want to run riot,
Or cause any playful chaos
That mostly they will do.
So I will whisper they like dancing
But that's between me and you.

Thus Beth likes the slow sensual
Movements of the waltz,
While Ted loves the flamboyance
Of a dramatic dance of course.
So while Beth will slink around
With Ted counting one, two, three,
He much prefers the lively tango
And cavorts for all to see.

But naturally they have to practice
And that is how I caught them out,
Sneaking in to see unnoticed
Both Ted's strut, and Beth's pout.

Though I made sure I wasn't caught
So can have another crafty look,
At those lovable, naughty bears
Learning their dancing from a book.
But meanwhile I love to tease them
And they don't know what to say,
When I creep up behind them
With a loud shout of "ole!"

--ooOoo–

Circus Clowns

Ted and Beth saw a circus advertised
And got tempted before I realised,
Their idea for having thrills and dares
Was to run away and be circus bears.

Now I'm not really sure about this
And I explained what they would miss,
When touring about in a circus bus
For Beth is known to make a fuss,
If everything isn't all neat and trim,
Getting cross with Ted, and blaming him
For being untidy and not putting away,
Things that he had used that day.

But despite my advice and explanation
They wanted to go straight to the station,
And join the nearest circus around
Not knowing where it could be found.

So I asked them what they would do
In a circus watched by me and you?
But they seemed to have really thought
About this, and wouldn't be caught.
For Ted says that taming lions is hip
And he is quite an expert with a whip,
Whilst Beth thinks she'll be an acrobat,
But Ted has grave doubts of that.

So he suggested that Beth could juggle
But we all know she'd rather snuggle,
Up with Ted and take life very easy
And not be circus travel queasy.

Though the pair of them were still sure
About being stars from the circus door,
With Ted saying he can fly trapeze
And even blindfolded will be at ease.
But Beth seemed very scared of this
Trying to distract him with a kiss,
While beginning to think a circus life
Could fuel her fears and strife.

So now I think they've changed their minds
And look for excitement of different kinds.
For circus life for them wouldn't be right
Because they like it very easy at night.
Thus I think they'll look for other things
Which a happiness to them brings.
And my laughing is now causing frowns
Teasing them being circus clowns.

--ooOoo–

Space Bears

Ted and Beth are keen on space travel
And both fancy being an astronaut,
Though as ever haven't thought it through
With all you need to do, and to be taught.
But all this has never worried our Ted
Who has a confidence big as a horse,
So just assumes he can easily do it
Which we know is wrong of course.

Now Beth she isn't always so sure
But will follow her Ted to the very end,
Whatever trouble it often gets her in
Or to the difficult places it can send.

So they have both contacted NASA
And put their training applications in,
Thus are now waiting very excitably
And can't wait for their career to begin.

But sadly life doesn't always work out
And no teddy bears have been in space,
So our bears are going to be disappointed
Although for them it is no disgrace,
Because when their bad news came back
Saying that neither had been selected,
Both were sent little teddy space suits
Which they hadn't really expected.

So now they are walking about proudly
Both with helmets firmly in place,
Along with their little teddy space suits
That sadly won't be worn up in space.
But of course we've come to know
Nothing much daunts our hero bears,
Who soon forgot the disappointment
Carrying on their lives without cares.

--ooOoo—

Ted and Beth's Fishing Trip

Ted decided that he would go fishing
As his plan to sail a boat had failed,
Because he and Beth had got worried
And as the tide was out hadn't sailed.

So now Ted is taking a reluctant Beth
To go and hopefully catch some fish,
But Beth isn't too enthralled with the idea
As it's not exactly what she would wish,
Spending time on a cold, wet river bank
While an enthusiastic Ted casts out his line.
For as usual he is all confident and sure,
But Beth's mood is not too sublime.

Especially when Ted give an angry shout
As he gets his line caught up in a tree,
Because although he brags and swaggers
It so often goes very wrong you'll see,
For now he can't free his his tangled line
However hard he pulls at it and tugs.
So he is angrily forced to give it up
Muttering teddy words as he shrugs.

So Beth says its best that they go home
But Ted won't hear of any such wish,
Saying he has got many other fishing lines
And will not go until catching some fish,
So the determined, cross look on his face
Fills our Beth with frustration and worry,
As she knows he might now stay all night
If he doesn't get a fish catching flurry.

Now unusually for them they start to argue
And Beth's patience is getting much shorter,
Until with an anguished and startled shout
Ted slips and falls into the muddy water,
Initially sending Beth into laughing hysterics
Seeing him soaking wet, with an angry frown,
But then her laughter turns into worried fear
As she panics her Ted could drown!

But Beth's helping paw aids Ted to get out
Although a much sadder and wiser bear,
Who is learning another painful lesson
About cockiness and him taking more care.
So unhappily our bears traipse off home
With Ted still in quite a little teddy strop,
But Beth knows just how to cheer him up
And buys fish and chips from a shop!

--ooOoo--

Fish and Chips

Now Ted n Beth are healthy bears
And they really like their food,
With me having to watch them
To ensure that they have chewed
And eaten their food properly,
In a dignified and appropriate way.
Because they can be very naughty
Whatever else they try to say!

Of course they will try to eat
Too many cakes and sugary sweets,
So I have to monitor them
To make sure that they're just treats.
For although often causing upsets
With the occasional little row,
They have come to understand
I look after them now.

Which brings us to their favourite
And that is fish and chips,
For the slightest mention of this
Will make them smack their lips.
So once again I try to ensure
They don't have it too regularly.
Because it's a very tempting meal,
Which also goes for me.

And that brought about a situation
When our bears felt a bit unrequited,
For I went to a fish and chips lunch
And they had not been invited.

So this did not go down well
When it was all arranged by phone.
And though they would come along
I went for fish and chips alone!
But as I tried to explain to them
And they had to finally agree,
Whilst loving and promoting them
They can't always come with me.

Thus now all is done and forgotten
With no more angry, teddy quips.
For I went right out and bought,
Their own meal of fish and chips!

--ooOoo—

FOOD & DRINK

Tripe and Onions

Tripe and onions, bangers and mash
Even spaghetti bog as well,
These are meals we love to have
But why do we have a need to tell
About everything we eat and drink
On news and social media's view?
For if that is not all enough
We have to see photos of it too.

Here is our lovely meal just served
Doesn't it all look rather grand,
With a photo of smiling faces
Just for fun you understand?
So now a full view of ordered meal
To be scoffed by the wild rovers,
And yes that we can just about take
But not the photos of your left overs.

With shots of half eaten bits of food
Or perhaps a plate that's almost clean.
As it was the best food ever you said,
As if we had all never been
Out for a meal or even a banquet
As that's how your description seems,
To us spectators on media logged
And seeing everybody's dreams.

Though I must admit to my cynicism
Like Mister Shakespeare's touch.
For if everything is so wonderful
Why do you have to say so much
About the very best of food
That only you seem to have had?
So come on you can't really believe,
We don't all think you a little sad?

--ooOoo–

Drunk Bingo Caller

Many people love their bingo
And closely watch their card,
Hoping that all the numbers
Getting called, is not too hard.
So they all listen intently
To the compare calling out,
Whilst fervently believing
They'll win without a doubt.

But possibly the worst event
Ensuring that hopes have shrunk.
Is coming to chilling recognition,
That the caller is blind drunk.
For he slurs the usual sayings
About two fat ladies free.
But instead of eighty-eight,
He calls out fifty-three!

Followed by another favourite
About being unlucky for some.
Though he doesn't call thirteen,
He shouts out number one!
So that's how it now continues
And punters aren't in heaven,
When he says it's number fifty
Instead of those legs eleven.

But by now he has been rumbled
And pulled quickly from the balls,
Before more ensuing chaos
From his drunken bingo calls,
That have all the fans in uproar
With a disruption never seen.
As he's clearly had more drinks,
Than that sweet sixteen!

--ooOoo—

Booze and Two's

It is written that alcohol increases desire
But reduces performance too,
This can be proved on most weekends
When the drunkards roll into view.

Inhibitions and balance both fade
The harder they drink and revel,
With love in the air and emotions high
And skirts raised to panties level,
On young ladies mostly so serene
And always shy of the sexy scrum.
But with lots of drink inside them now
They're more than keen to flash their bum!

Blokes also will feel the effect
As more alcohol lowers their wit.
They think they're great lovers and Romeo's
But in truth most are not even fit.
Though that doesn't stop them at all
Trying to show off all their might,
With them struggling to just stand up
Let alone trying to fight.

Yes alcohol can always take its toll
Making a fool out of me and you,
For I've never been to bed with an ugly girl
But woken up with quite a few!

--ooOoo—

All Wrapped Up

I can't open up the wrapper
No matter how hard I try.
Like undoing a peanut packet,
A big tug and out they fly!

Pull here, the packet glibly says
So there you pull but have no joy.
And the pouch stays firmly shut
As you pull and tug it like a toy.

Biscuits tightly wrapped are fun
When the opening tag won't work.
And the biscuits are now crumbs
As the packet you pull and jerk.

The cereal box says open here
So you dutifully aim to comply.
But hard luck, it's open other end,
So you just scream and cry!

Whatever type of wrapper cover
Is between you and your wares,
It will set up a conundrum test
Sure to give you bad nightmares.

If your goods don't have a tag pull
They'll be mummified all in tape,
That will hurt and break your nails
Leaving you with a puzzled gape.

So best be prepared for opening war
And arm yourself with all the tools,
Scissors, hammer, knife and bombs
For this package fight has no rules!

--ooOoo--

Have Another Beer

The weather is not great
And through the rain we peer,
It is getting us all down
So have another beer.

We want to drive away
But roads are blocked I hear,
There are far too many cars
So let's have another beer.

A trip up to the shops
To join the thronging crowd,
And mad folks with their trolleys
Make you want to curse aloud!
So you stay at home to book
A holiday, not too dear,
But the internet is down
Best to have another beer.

Then you're on the phone
Many options now to choose,
It's enough to drive you mad
And go back on the booze.
They say you're in a queue
But your turn is nowhere near,
I can't be doing this
So I'll have another beer.

Thus there's so many things
In life to drive you mad,
So have another beer then
You just won't feel so bad!

--ooOoo—

Spot of Bother

A crispy blouse or clean white shirt
Are almost certain to attract the dirt,
So however hard you try not to be rude
You will still blot your top with food,
That you observe with great dismay
For it will always happen that way.

But some food types that you chose
Are guaranteed to spoil your clothes,
With a spot here, or a splash there
Despite your best attempts at care,
For with some food it's best to be petty
Like that messy, tricky spaghetti.

So when spruced up so smart and clean
You will make mess that's easily seen,
With blobs and slops down your front
The poorest eyesight won't need to hunt.
And the more you rub and wipe the stain
It will look much worse and still remain.

But men have a problem very grave
If hurrying too much when they shave,
And nick themselves, though not too big
It will still bleed like a stuck pig,
So that you wish you'd left off your top
When your bleeding refuses to stop,
And now you're due to go smartly out
So that being on time is a big doubt.
As you must rapidly change your attire
Your readiness now goes down to the wire,
Till at last again all dressed to thrill
But any chance to stay clean is virtually nil.

--ooOoo—

Handfight at the OK Sauce Table

Like the famous gunfight at OK corral
That was decided by superior force,
We can have our very own battle
If wanting to use the OK Sauce.

For their bottles can put up a fight
And be determined to frustrate you,
By refusing to serve smoothly
Whatever you try to do.
Because if the sauce is in there
It just won't come out the top.
Until you squeeze it in temper,
And then it just won't stop.

So you are faced with a meal
Covered with sauce now spread,
All over your waiting food
Which makes you lose your head,
And rant in a foul temper
In front of friends and those,
Who are now trying not to laugh
At your spattered plate and clothes.

Thus it may be time to withdraw
Or just quietly sit back down,
Gingerly trying to clear the mess
And attempt to smile, not frown.

Until a waiter comes to the rescue
As if summoned by a desperate bid,
Not to fall apart in embarrassment
When he calmly unscrews the lid,
Of the bottle you tried to squash
That didn't need squeezing at all.
For the bottle had a twist action,
So you're a sauce spattered fool!

--ooOoo—

The Lonely Life of a Lemon

The poor old lemon has a lonely life
Because it can never win it seems,
Despite adding taste to many drinks
As from the glass it gleams.

But very few own up to lemon liking
It is one of those unwritten laws,
For a lemon has some connotations
That are associated with dull bores,
Also it has quite a thick skin
With a very sour and acidic taste.
So being seen as, or called a lemon
Is not a great thing to be faced.

For anybody who is called a lemon
Is meant to be an unsatisfactory type
Or of defective or feeble nature,
Although that may be just the hype.
Because lemons do have their uses
In the culinary world and for cleaning,
So before writing the poor lemon off
You better check on its meaning.

For lemons are popular in cooking
And go to make lemon meringue pie,
Which is a favourite of many people
So can cause a glint in their eye.
And let's not forget the lemon curd
That is appreciated by folks too,
So it seems downsides of lemons
May not always be totally true.

Though of course we must understand
How the lemon can stand alone.
As it has quite a sour taste to it
So can mean people who like to moan,
As are often referred to as a lemon
Or thick skinned according to some.
But best beware of their acid side
As they may have a bite at your bum.

Thus the much maligned sad lemon
Hasn't really done too much wrong,
To cause it to be ostracised and lonely
And kept from the smiling throng.

--ooOoo—

DRESS & ATTIRE

No Hiding Place

At our local swimming pool
You can see many a curious sight.
With lots of lovely young girls,
Whilst other scenes are a fright.

Men wearing tight fitting trunks,
"Budgie Smugglers" for the thin.
Though sadly worn by some "largies"
Having more hanging out, than in!
For it seems a life contradiction
That the larger many folk grow,
Instead of tucking it safely away
They must put it all out on show.

Now I'm not against big sizes
I have a growing waist myself,
But I fervently try to hide it
Not put it on the front shelf.

But back to those swimming trunks
Of varying size of modesty cover,
And the battle of those bulges
Where some really need another
Or much larger piece of cloth,
To keep their harvest all intact.
For hiding mountains behind a stamp
Won't work, and that's a fact!

--ooOoo—

Sunrise Strip

The weather is getting better
And sunshine is coming back,
Which surely heralds the return
Of the famous builders crack,
That greets us from their shorts
Failing to gather everything in.
Looking terrible on the large
And not much better on the thin.

Now our rare sunshine is the cue
For awful sights, if I can be blunt,
With bums showing at the back
And bellies hanging out the front.
Though our builder or tradesman does
Go to work with all his might,
But sadly in too small shorts
That allows rock bottom sight.

Another grotesque view we get
Seen in towns of grit and dirt,
Is when the suns rays come out
The blokes must remove their shirt.
And if that's not bad enough
With exposure of their belly flops,
They disgustingly walk round like it
Inside our stores and shops.

So that is some of the problems
When out the sunshine comes,
Though folks enjoying it is good to see
But not a close up of their bums.
Now I'm not a model icon
Sure my body has it its flaws,
But if exhibitionists can't cover up
It's far best they stay indoors!

--ooOoo—

Black Socks

The guy was all ready for the sun
I mean this man had it all.
A shirt to find your way home with,
With shorts just a bit too small.
A baseball cap perched on his head
While a neck chain said he rocks,
He had a smashing pair of sandals
But Oh, with jet black socks!

These were pulled high up his legs
Right beyond his calf,
So despite all your best efforts
You couldn't help but laugh.
Now I'm not against black socks
Of course they have their place.
In black shoes and dark trousers,
But in sandals they're a disgrace.

So our man swaggered in the sun
Taking off his trendy hat,
Revealing scant hair but a pony tail
Hanging on his shoulder like a rat.
Now I really don't wish to be cruel
But it was this that made me wail,
Though a close call belly laugh
Between black socks and pony tail.

Though we do live in a free country
And can wear what you will or won't,
But with black socks in open sandals
It's far better that you don't !!!

--ooOoo–

The Witch

The witch flew on her flightpath
When her bra all turned to dust.
It didn't affect her flying
But it played havoc with her bust!

She had to make an instant landing
As she looked a grisly sight.
So tied one boob up to the left
And swung the other to her right.

Then cursing her ample bosom
That dropped down to her crutch,
She reflected on the saying
More than a mouthful is too much

--ooOoo—

Leggings Don't Tell Lies

There are many varied clothing items
For men and women, large and small,
But these can be fraught with danger
For some you shouldn't wear at all.

Well that is if you are larger
And maybe ate too many pies,
So be careful with what you choose ,
For those leggings don't tell lies.
Because they're invariably tight fitting
And not so easy to get over thighs,
Giving a too-small-for-you picture
As those leggings won't tell lies.

For even if you pull them high
Over your legs and up your belly,
There is not any hiding places
So your middle shakes like a jelly.
And anyway I just can't work it out
If you have a fuller figure size,
Why people won't get extra large
Because leggings don't tell lies.

So on and on the struggle goes
Just like the battle of the bulge,
But by wearing those tight leggings
All your large areas you divulge.
For if you must wear figure hugging
It's far better that you get wise,
And don't go near tight britches
Because leggings don't tell lies.

Though of course we all like to try
Various fashions that catch our eyes,
And it is very easy to get caught
So remember leggings won't tell lies.

But please don't despair too much
If your body is large with flaws,
Go ahead and wear what you want,
But probably best you stay indoors!

--ooOoo—

Zipping Up

Zip fasteners are so amazing
They have you done up in a trice,
But if they don't line up right
You may be trying more than twice.
Because like little things at times
They won't work and "get your goat",
So you could be idly standing there
Pulling angrily at your coat!

For zips can catch inner linings
Or side material of your clothes,
And unless you zip up correctly
Your frustration and anger shows,
With this aggravating small device
That slides up and down like grease,
Or leaves you baffled and fuming
As you lose your inner peace!

But for men though, there is danger
When they're zipping up their fly.
They must ensure all is tucked in,
Or they will give a piercing cry.
For nothing is so extremely painful
And can make your eyeballs whip,
If any stray bit of hair or tackle
Gets caught up in the zip!

So now we have seen both sides
Of the quick and neat zip slider,
That's so easy to make all secure
So clothes won't gape open any wider.
But we must ensure we zip up right
With fasteners lined up with care,
And reduce any risk of it snagging
To save clothes from wear and tear!

--ooOoo—

Dress Sense

There is a tricky problem
To avoid an awkward sight,
When men consider their dressing
On the left or to the right.
So choice of clothing is important
And they mustn't be too tight,
Or you will be clearly showing
If you prefer the left or right.

But baggy trousers aren't the answer
Even if you are contrite.
For loose fittings may well choose
If you're going left or right.
Or may even cause a nuisance
And perhaps a concerning fight,
If attempting to stay central
And not on left or right.

Thus for men to feel more relaxed
With non-worrying delight,
They must have a confidence
Of not causing sudden fright,
With an accidental display
Even if it's only very slight,
So all must firmly be in place
To the left or to the right.

Though now in enlightened times
Where rules are black and white,
You shouldn't get into trouble
Or put anyone to flight.
In fact possibly the opposite
Which can make your future bright,
If your dressing is more obvious
And brings an invite for the night.

--ooOoo—

Syrups

My head is completely bald
Well I shave the bit not dead.
But I could never walk around
With a cheap syrup on my head!

Even the most expensive wig
Won't have anybody fooled,
That it's a healthy head of hair
And that's without it being pulled.

For most syrup of figs are obvious
As to what exactly is up there,
So no colouring or grooming
Can make it look like Barnet Fair.
And I would be more embarrassed
With a bit of carpet on my head,
Than with my bald shining dome
Hidden by a silly cloth instead!

But it's not that you can't notice
A sort of birds nest sitting flat,
That doesn't match or fit right
Like some tatty doorstep mat!

For going bald is quite natural
Most men will at least lose some,
Even the men who kept their hair
Wonder how they didn't succumb!

So most blokes I know are derisive
Of wig wearing guys, so vain,
And our best advice to the "wiggies"
Is to throw your money down the drain!

--ooOoo—

Fun From Crisis

It often seems out of an awful crisis
That comical things can still arise,
Perhaps not so much for everyone
But mostly amusing in my eyes.
For right now we have a killer virus
So no laughing at this tragedy it's true,
As it has turned the world upside down
By changing nearly everything we do.

But people will all react differently
And some take precautions to the bone,
To protect themselves from this menace
And develop a style all of their own.

Like the chap I saw waiting in a queue
With a tatty looking mask on his face,
That maybe could have been excused
But not the Aussie style hat with lace,
Sewed all around the turned up edges
To make my eyes pop out on stalks,
For the only thing that it had missing
Was a bobbing row of dangling corks.

Another view that alerted my attention
With a glance and smothered smile,
As an attractive lady in a floral dress
Had a patterned mask in great style,
Clearly having taken some matching
To look just right without a doubt,
But not for a fairly empty Tesco store
And perhaps more for a big night out.

Though obviously we must take seriously
A silent killer causing coughs like pepper,
But some people move aside in courtesy
And others treat everyone like a leper,

So if we must endure this awful curse
That has closed pubs, bars and stores,
And subjected us to weird behaviour
Maybe it is best that we stay indoors.

For I cannot always stop my humour
And guarantee my mouth stays shut,
When people cavort about the street
In ill fitting clothes and a crap hair cut,
Undoubtedly done in a panic by a partner
Shocked by how long the hair had grown,
Thus had attempted to tidy it all up
But clearly should have left well alone.

--ooOoo—

TECHNOLOGY

Bogged Down

A visit to that smallest room
Where you normally go alone,
Or maybe have a secret tryst
With your precious mobile phone,
Can now be laced with dangers
That can wreak havoc on a soul,
If carelessly or without intent
You drop the mobile in the bowl.

For no matter how quickly acting
To get this important item back,
From its soaking down the toilet
And any motions you now lack,
Will not prevent serious damage
Caused by water, before unseen
And sadly now dawning on you,
For there's nothing on the screen.

So you desperately try to save,
This mini computer with its store
Of contacts and information,
Which unhappily show no more.

Thus extreme measures are needed
Although some are not too nice,
For common myths suggests it helps
If you smother the phone with rice,
Before wrapping it up very warm
And putting it in the airing cupboard,
To hope for a little miracle of joy
A bit like Old Mother Hubbard.

But eventually with a heavy heart
You now have to accept the fate,
Of dropping the phone in the bowl
And trying to rescue it too late.

For mobile phones and toilet seats
Don't make a very happy pair.
So you have learnt a hard lesson
Not to take your next one there.
Because another phone is needed
To survive in this day and age.
So ensure to take great care of it
And prevent another toilet rage.

--ooOoo—

Who Goes There?

Remembering passwords can be hard
And also a user name too,
Before gaining any access
On technology owned by you.

But you tap in with a confidence
The word needed to log in,
Though sadly it comes up "error"
For this battle you won't win.
So you try again, so sure you're right
By putting in your word name.
This will surely be the one
But the failure's just the same.

"Forgotten your password?" flashes up
And through gritted teeth you hiss,
"No of blooming course not"
I just like playing this
Stupid and annoying game,
Before I can check my screen
And read all my information,
Though it looks like I'm too keen!

Change your password on here then
And all will be right for you,
But you will need to add your
User name, before this you do,
And successfully pass this test,
That's now making you see red.
So you bash your keys in anger
And watch the screen go dead.

"Oh most holy gosh and bother"
You mutter under your breath,
Knowing that it's all your fault
That caused the lap top's death.
For it doesn't want to respond
Whatever trick you try to use,
So it seems like poetic justice
If technology you abuse.

A journey to the repairers
Is now a trip you must make,
Confessing or not your guilt
You had more than you could take,
In dealing with requirements
Of all security names and text,
That you thought would be easy
But you forgot what came next.

So if there is an answer to all this
And to not look like a clown,
It's to say bugger their advice
And write your passwords down!

--ooOoo--

Coffee Capers

The coffee machine lurks ominously
In many a canteen, cafe or bar,
Waiting for use by the unwary
Though they won't get very far.

For these coffee dispensers are computers
Or they may just as well be thus,
As they baffle many a would be user
Who should work them without fuss.
But these things have a devil side,
That reduce many to unhappy fears
Of frustration at their incompetence
To get some coffee without tears.

So go boldly up to them and serve
Yourself coffee as marked by the guide,
To uncertain victims putting cups down
Who watch as the coffee pours outside
Of that awaiting cup of yours
Placed just where told you "oughta".
But when you push the button again
It only fills your cup with water!

But this only happens if you can see
How you think this conundrum works,
For there are many levers and taps
That all have their different quirks.
So you just stand in embarrassment
And shame not knowing what to do,
But fear not for there is consolation
As most are beaten just like you.

--ooOoo—

Pardon?

Can't take your call at the moment
The metallic voice intones,
And will repeat this basic sentence
Every time that someone phones.
Please leave your message then
After you hear the beep,
So that we can get back to you
And this promise they will keep.

Well, that is on the condition
That you got their number right,
For metallic lady could be anyone
As no name, or face was in sight.
Thus I'm sure I'm not alone
In leaving a message for reply,
To someone that I didn't know
Who will sit and wonder why!

For I like to hear a real voice
Perhaps recorded by a friend,
Or a person saying who you rang
At the phones other end,
For a posh, plastic recording
Could be anyone wrongly dialled,
So now I will always ring again
Ensuring the number is re trialled.

Though it doesn't just end there,
For when the person rings you back
You could be out or busy,
So your voice they will lack.
And so your message will talk to them
Just as theirs had spoken to you,
For if you want to feel important
This is what you need to do.

So sometimes in a few minutes
You could ring many different folk,
And get all their answer-phones
Which really is a joke.
For you must await a return call,
But perhaps all this was staged,
For if you try to ring again,
That number's now engaged.

Thus on and on it all goes round
A circle of messages in a store.
But by then you've had enough
And metallic lady's the last straw!

--ooOoo—

Social Distance Zapper

Since Coronavirus we have all been told
To social distance over two metres apart,
But that doesn't always seem to work
As some folk just won't play their part,
Which can lead us into temptation
If they crowd us, awkward like a crab.
The fat, the thin and even some small
Are then most deserving of our jab.

For if standing in a queue, or just passing
People still seem to invade your space,
Thus you need to give them a reminder
Of their distance failure and disgrace.

So when I heard about this new device
A "Social Distance Zapper" you can use,
I didn't really have much of a problem
In thinking of people I would choose,
To give out a sharp little reminder
If coming too close into my trap,
And get them to move rapidly away
When I gave them one up with my zap!

Now of course this can lead to conflict
When you play your "zapper" card,
So you may need to quickly say to them
They must stay away at least one yard,
And give you your social distance space
With a healthy area of mutual respect,
For if they fail, or agree to observe this
A zapping shock they can expect.

But naturally we must be very careful
To only use our zapper as we are taught,
For I have a fear we may end up in trouble
And on a "charge" of common assault.
Though this may all prove worthwhile
If educating the non-compliant or the bold,
So may be deserving of a zap reminder
Until they learn to do as they are told!

--ooOoo—

Three's Tease

They say things happen in threes
I've heard that said before,
But if bad things happen with ease
I don't want to play any more!

For if incidents can easily total two
So are likely to descend on me,
Thus giving me plenty more to do
Without another making it three!

Two's company, three is a crowd,
I heard someone give that advice.
But if making a mistake out loud
I won't want to make it twice.

For I think the saying that two
Is more romantic than a trio,
To get love on with me and you
Only needs one more Taurus or Leo.
But if we can make our love sane
I'm told that we can make another,
Which brings us back to the start again,
Now three with a new sister or brother.

Though if big trouble comes along
With a need for fight to stay alive,
If up against an angry throng
Your company's better numbering five!

--ooOoo—

Bump Hump

Nothing is more certain sure
To give me the real "mint lump,"
Than getting bounced and rattled
By an oversized speed bump!

They seem now to have multiplied
And spread as weeds on a lawn,
So however you try to avoid them
Your chances are quite forlorn.
Large ones and some wide types
Even the narrow little bars,
No matter how you cross them
They ensure each muscle jars!

Yes I know that they're for safety
And to slow fast drivers down,
But they bunch the traffic up too
So you will always get the clown,
Who tries to miss them out,
Swerving on your side of the road
As if some right of free passage
Was just on him bestowed.

So we're lumbered with these bumps
Which seem as big as hills,
That crash you down the other side
Just like roller coaster thrills.
For whatever technique you try
To negotiate these barricades,
Driving very slowly or diagonally
Your frustration just cascades.

So accept them as we must
For they are surely here to stay,
Or just seek diversions round them
That may take forever and a day!

--ooOoo—

No Entry

There's a gremlin in my lap top
Who reads my every word,
And causes little glitches
Whilst I have hardly stirred.

It sits watching all my typing
So when the last word is near,
There is a flicker on the screen
And my work will all disappear.

Now any attempt to retrieve it
Makes gremlin laugh and scoff,
For each time I touch the panel
He turns the damn thing off!

Though I have a perfect signal
And connection speed is great,
Still my little Genie gremlin
Says my "save as" was too late.

Now my full battery sign is on
So all's well, and off I go,
To try to get the work back
But my reaction time is slow.

So I need to start off thinking
What can this gremlin be?
But I have an uneasy feeling
It is all blooming down to me!

--ooOoo—

Appendix

Kind compliments and feedback to me on my poetry increases as I continue to write and produce more books, number nine now, but it still recounts that many people like to work out the meanings of my poems for themselves, or even attach their own personal experiences and thoughts as they resonate with them.

I think that is truly wonderful, but for other folks who like to seek my reasons and explanations for them my poems, please review my comments below.

As I tend to write spontaneously and often on subjects that have really emoted me, I will mostly "nail my thoughts in", so most of the themes are quite clear or self-explanatory.

However, the poems listed in this appendix below are the less obvious topics and thoughts, but please attach any personalisation or special meaning that they have for you individually, because I will feel really honoured if you do!

Bar Room Star:

Sentimental early favourite of mine as it was published in a national daily newspaper.

Cocky Two's:

Pub inhabitants who sat perched at the bar, blocking it to everyone else trying to get served, whilst also spouting off.

A Little Loud:

Similar to "Bar Room Star" but notable for an immense noise from a small person.

Chariot Wheels:

Frustration of shopping whilst dodging unaware people endangering others with their poor trolly control.

Left Turn Loons:

On selfish and thoughtless drivers, particularly those not using indicators.

Nellie and I:

Another account of an actual occurrence involving me.

Guardian Angel:

On an old joke and saying of mine if I had "mucked up"

Toilet Rolls:

An actual take on life in early 2020 with people panic buying.

Sample:

Experiences of an essential health check that can be fraught with difficulties.

O M G:

My thinly veiled frustrations with a continual banal exclamation.

First Sex Lessons:
Looking back at my intriguing improvisations for lack of formal sex education.

Tripe and Onions:
My comments about people posting photos of their food and even leftovers on social media.

Hand Fight at OK sauce table:
My parody of the gunfight at the OK corral, (but this has actually happened).

The Lonely Life of a Lemon:
As most people will have "felt like a lemon" at some time, why do we ostracise them? This is my plea for lemons then.

Black Socks:
One of my pet hates and amusements.

The Witch:
My caustic response to a cartoon sent to me.

Dress Sense:
On problems of comfort and decorum.

Who Goes There?:
My frustration with technology and trying to "log in".

Coffee Capers:
The trauma and trials of using coffee machines.

Pardon:
My frustration with answerphones, especially if they don't say who you've rung.

More?

I hope that you enjoyed this book
For I tried to pack lots in,
With various themes in sections
So you can choose where to begin,
And take yourself on journeys
Or if you wished to, just remain.
For I have other books out now,
Thus you can have it all again.

With poems to make you romantic
And some verses if you feel deep.
Others will make you look back on life,
Even smile when you go to sleep.

Of course Ted and Beth will feature
I can hardly leave them out.
As surely they'll have new adventures,
Well of this I have no doubt!
And I will have new observations
I glean from scanning life's tree.
Take care then you are not included
When I write down what I see.

So please look at my other books
And support "Help for Heroes" too,
For all my sales donate to them
From my poems I write for you.

You can get books from my website online
And to message me direct will be fine.
With every contact listed below
Including all that you need to know,
To search for me on the Amazon club
Or just come and find me down the pub!

My other books are:-

Poetic Views of Life
MORe Poetic Views of Life
Reviews of Life in Verse
Life Scene in Verse
Life Presented in Verse
Poet Reveals All
Poet Reflects Your World
Poetic Seeds to Fruition
Our World in Verse

My Contacts:-
Email = lw1800@hotmail.co.uk
Amazon authors page= Laurie Wilkinson
Facebook page = The Psychy Poet Laurie Wilkinson
Facebook page =Ted n Beth of Laurie the Poet
Website = www.lauriewilkinson.com

Printed in Great Britain
by Amazon

69093963R00112